C000081419

Margaret Thatcher

A Margaret Thatcher Biography

Michael Woodford

Table of Contents

"The Iron Lady"

One of the most famous figures in world history was a grocer's daughter who clawed her way to the top of her country's political hierarchy.

At a time when women had defined roles in society and had to grapple with barriers and glass ceilings because of their sex, ambitious and fiery Margaret Hilda Roberts – later, Prime Minister Margaret Thatcher - somehow became (for all of its good and bad) the groundbreaking, trailblazing "Iron Lady."

She did not consider her background or her sex to be a weakness. In fact, she transformed them into a unique proposition. She transformed them into strengths on her way to becoming Europe's first female Prime

Minister. They became part of her brand and iconography, and she sold the sometimes bitter pill of her tough politics with her characteristics.

Britain in the 1970s

Britain in the late-1970s was grappling with many political, economic and cultural changes. Decades of affluence post-war had given way to a nation struggling to compete on the world stage. It was not one of the country's finer moments, and there was a sense of it being a declining empire.

Memories of those years past are notoriously bleak, and Margaret Thatcher – whether justly or unjustly – is often credited for national salvation. David Cameron, Prime Minister from 2010 to 2016, honored Margaret Thatcher with a bold tribute stating she "*didn't just lead…she saved our country.*" It is a sentiment held by many.

Before she came into the office, inflation was in double-digits and taking a huge chunk out of the value of people's earnings. When she became Prime Minister in 1979, inflation was at 10.3 percent per year.

There were crippling strikes aplenty from trade unions. 1.4 million people – 5.3 percent of the workforce – did not have jobs in 1979. State-owned industries were not at their most efficient. When she came to power, the state had ownership and control in the industries of coal, electricity, gas, petroleum, steel, telecom and water. Government debt was high too, at 43.6 percent of GDP in 1979.

Margaret Thatcher set to work controlling runaway inflation. She withstood striking unions and in one famous case, called their bluff and did not blink for a year until they gave up. Her government worked on union reform. Her policies helped shift her country from the manufacturing industry to services.

Her free market vision privatized many industries.

Many of the changes she made were so profound that they were regarded as irreversible, inherited by the governments that succeeded hers, and the effects of which are still apparent up to now.

Loved and Hated

The results of her 11 years in office actualizing her stern, self-reliant, some say individualistic worldview leave her with a mixed legacy.

For her critics, trade union reform left unions practically impotent and the working class with less bargaining power over corporations. Deregulation led to reckless and risky financial behavior that has repeatedly endangered whole economies. Many communities dependent on manufacturing lost their main source of livelihood and never fully recovered. Some critics even blame her and the loyal proponents of her Thatcherism for crafting a country divided both in rhetoric as well as in economic class.

Many people felt left behind, even when the economy was recovering and corporations were excelling. Some felt the working classes were bearing the bitter pill of her sweeping reforms while the rich were less burdened.

Her complex politics eventually led to protests on the streets, divisions within her own party and eventually, her resignation.

Love her or hate her, what cannot be denied is that Margaret Thatcher inherited a tough situation and she had to be tough right back in pretty much every imaginable respect – in the climb to her position, the maintenance of her position, and in doing the actual work of attempting to improve her country's condition. She was patriotic and hard-working, often having 18-hour days. She also paid the price in sacrificing irrecoverable time and close relationships with her family.

Indeed, given all the costs, the Prime Minister's job can be considered a bitter prize for the precious few who could win it.

British politics was still an old boys' club when Margaret Hilda Roberts came into the picture. She had her taste of rejections and defeats, and the wins when they finally came did not come easy. All the while she had to face double standards, suffering personal attacks aside from fending off those lobbied against her politics.

She was considered frosty, abrasive and combative, where a male politician would have likely just gotten away with firmly asserting his will. Comments were made on her hair, on her clothes, on her voice. As one Conservative commenter was quoted by

Time in 1975, she was *"the wrong sort of woman."*

Her work also took a toll on her personal life. When she came into power in 1979, she was married and a mother of twins. Her demanding work would present challenges and lost opportunities for bonding with her family, especially with her children.

As for her beloved husband, being married to one of the most powerful women in the world could not have been easy, on top of his own concerns as a millionaire businessman. At some point, their union was even be plagued by rumors of the possibility of a divorce.

Indeed, it was not easy being an "Iron Lady" at the pinnacle of British politics on the world stage. Margaret Thatcher had to leap fences and defy the odds at almost every step of the way.

As we all know, her unlikely ascension to power was only the beginning. She also had to push a bold, broad vision for her country that was not uncontroversial (to say the least!), and would lead her people to irreversible changes.

Her politics and economics of small government, privatization, deregulation and self-reliance courted and still courts strenuous opposition, and she had to make hard calls in hard times.

But even her critics would have to admit that she had courage and cunning, and she helped usher in some much-needed modernity to struggling segments of the economy.

Her name would eventually be given to a modern and powerful political philosophy that still carries a certain appeal in our present time: Thatcherism.

All but a few politicians in all the countries of the world can boast of having a trademark vision, captured in a single word.

She, in short, made history.

This is hers.

The Early Years

Everyone had to start from somewhere. But for a woman who spent 11 years at the much-coveted address of 10 Downing Street sitting on the hard-won Prime Minister seat, the unlikely beginnings could be found in a politically-active grocer's home in the market town of Grantham.

Childhood and Faith

Margaret Hilda Roberts was born on the 13th of October, 1925 in Grantham, Lincolnshire, England. She was the daughter of shopkeeper, Methodist lay preacher and alderman (later, mayor) Alfred Roberts and his wife, Beatrice. The family lived above the shop, where Margaret was sometimes spotted behind the counter.

Alfred Roberts was a powerful influence in Margaret's life. She credited him for *"all the things that I do believe."* At 6 feet and 3 inches tall with a voice made for sermons, he cut a striking speaker, and had actually toured Methodist circles for sermons. Margaret was often with him.

Her home life and the father who headed it, shaped much of the "iron" character the world would eventually come to know. The Methodist faith followed by the family and preached by her father has even been regarded by some political and religious pundits as the roots of "Thatcherism."

While this may sound surprising, it should be noted that one of the most famous quotes attributed to Margaret Thatcher is, *"Economics is the method; the object is to change the soul."* She also described in an interview that the underlying foundation of a democracy is not only the vote of a majority but beyond that, into morality – *"the belief that the majority of people are good and decent."* In short, there was a spiritual component to the way she looked at the world and how she governed her country.

But before she had her chance to meddle with the "method" as a Prime Minister, she lived with her family in a close-knit community and they were active in a congregation espousing shared values of free will, self-help and social involvement.

A typical Sunday for the Roberts sisters (Margaret and older sister Muriel), for example, comprised of both religious instruction and services, with restrictions on games and entertainment (even sewing!).

Beyond Sundays – for the future PM would say in an interview that her faith was not *"only a faith for Sundays,"* they also had social events around the congregation like the Youth Guild, and were raised on daily cleanliness, discipline, and duty. They prayed before and after eating, and were teetotalers. The woman who eventually became Prime Minister though, would later frequently enjoy whisky, which she found energizing and fortifying.

Either way, their faith was therefore a very deep, important and regular part of their lives.

Margaret's father Alfred Roberts, an in-demand lay preacher, had actually delivered sermons against avarice and extolled the values of thrift, self-reliance and a good work ethic. He also had distinct views on the freedom of the individual – which likely had a bearing on Margaret Thatcher's eventual belief in a free market. Methodism, after all, was a religion that the future PM would describe as a practical as well as an evangelical faith.

Her family's religious background and its belief in the individual – that the person's faith and accountability is ultimately between him and his God, that the Ten Commandments were addressed to individuals rather than collectives, that choices and actions should be left to the individual rather than to a larger body like the state - was not at odds with capitalism if pursued with altruism. She once noted there was nothing wrong in wealth creation; instead, what was wrong was in *the love of money...*"

Having funds after all, was what allowed a person to share in the first place. The founder of Methodism, John Welsey, was known for promoting hard work, thriftiness and saving, so that one may have the resources with which to be generous to the needy.

Margaret Thatcher's individualistic approach is also probably why in her later career, she was personally conservative but generally hands-off in matters that can be considered as areas of personal morality and conscience. Among these are divorce, abortion and sexuality.

Her faith also likely shaped her stance in the era's cause *du jour* – the Cold War. Communism after all, had been more about the state rather than the individual, and was not moved by faith in a god. She stood against communism abroad and against socialism on the domestic front, in what many look upon as a believable extension of her religious belief in individual liberty.

Margaret Thatcher's politics did not always align with Methodism along the course of her more than 11-year tenure as Prime Minister of course, and she later drifted closer to the formality of Anglicanism. Though some do say the shift may have been political, what with Tories being more linked with the Anglicans.

At any rate, as can be noted above, strokes of her father and their Methodist beliefs could be seen in the formation of the character and world view of the future Prime Minister.

Her perspectives were also likely formed by the harsh circumstances in which she and her community lived.

Her country was still coming from the ravages of the Great War of 1914-1918, and leading up to the Second World War which eventually broke out in 1939. There was peace by the time she turned 20 years old in 1945, but many men had been killed and there was also unemployment. But she, her family, their community and their country, just had to work hard and find a way to move forward.

Her childhood in Grantham imbued in her a sense of community, good neighborliness and civic duty and pride, which she would carry with her into her political career.

Education and Work Experience

Margaret Thatcher studied in state schools several miles away from home, which she walked to even as a young girl. She was a good student and got into Oxford University when she was 18 years old.

She had a fine, scientific mind. Her educational background was in Chemistry, which she studied at Somerville College in Oxford. One of her professors was the Nobel Prize winner, Dorothy Hodgkin.

Studying wasn't all she did at university, however. She became active in the Wesley Memorial chapel and lent her voice to preaching, but later became more active in politics. She cut her teeth at the Oxford University Conservative Association, which she eventually spearheaded as president (not the first female to do so, however; she was the third). Her involvement in the association allowed her to make Conservative connections that served her political career later.

She continued to be active in politics after graduation. Even when she moved to Colchester and was employed by a plastics company, she was still linked with the local organization of the Conservative Party. She also worked in the field of chemistry in Dartford.

Interestingly, Margaret Thatcher may be best known for her politics, but she also has another achievement. She, as part of a team at a chemistry company, helped develop ice cream additives and emulsifiers that made soft serve possible. Margaret Thatcher ultimately earned a reputation for being frigid, but it might surprise people to know she was involved in literal ice cream too!

First Political Forays

Her initial forays into elected office were unsuccessful. She became a prospective Conservative candidate for Dartford in Kent in 1949, but lost in the general elections of 1950 and 1951. It was at any rate, considered a "safe" Labour seat, a fact the savvy young pol was aware of but nevertheless fought through.

A community's party leanings wasn't her only challenge. She was young and a woman, where politics was male-dominated. But while the runs were unsuccessful, they increased her public profile. She wasn't just a promising young female; she was at the time, the *youngest* Conservative candidate ever. Margaret Roberts was a good story the media couldn't help but follow.

It wasn't just media attention that she gleaned from the unsuccessful initial forays into elected office. These also provided the encounters by which she would catch the eye of businessman, Denis Thatcher.

Love and Family

Denis Thatcher was born on the 10th of May, 1910 in Lewisham, London, England. The family's roots however, go back to the coastal town of Wanganui in New Zealand.

There, his grandfather made a fortune on weed killers for the railways. His father then put up a similar business endeavor in the U.K. for general chemicals and married a fellow entrepreneur, Lillian Bird.

Denis was sent to boarding school from age 8, first at Bognor Regis and then to Mill Hill. He wasn't the most remarkable of scholars, but excelled in sports like cricket and rugby.

He eventually finished school and headed off for work in the family business.

Even with his family at the helm, he was expected to work his way to the top. One of his duties brought him to Germany in 1937, where he got the sense that World War II was brewing.

When hostilities began exactly as he had expected them to, he was an army officer. He was, however, on the staff side due to poor eyesight. But by 1945 he was a Major at the British HQ in Marseilles, and had distinguished himself enough to be made a Member of the Order of the British Empire.

He also managed to get married and divorced…

His wife, the trailblazing Margaret Thatcher wasn't always the first in everything. The first Mrs. Denis Thatcher was Ms. Margaret Kempson, a beauty Denis wed in March

1942. They, however, never had the chance to live together because of the war and were divorced by 1948.

Denis thrived in the army, but left post-war to head his family's business. When his father fell ill in 1949, he became the managing director.

He met the spirited Margaret Roberts, then an Oxford research chemist, along the course of a dinner dance in 1950.

He was attracted to her and aside from his character, was a successful businessman and a millionaire as well – he had his own appeal. He was however divorced, with a known taste for gin. Not quite the Methodist poster boy, but his business acumen and some say resemblance to Margaret's father, eventually won her over too. He proposed in 1951 and she said yes. They married at Wesley's Chapel in London that year.

It may be recalled that this was also the year of her failed second try at entering parliament. But in gaining Denis Thatcher as a partner for life, she was blessed. He had the self-possession and confidence in his own assets and achievements to be comfortable being married to a powerful and ambitious woman. He also had the financial means to allow her to focus on her political career and take it to the next level.

After marriage, they honeymooned in Madeira, Paris and Portugal. She then studied law in 1952 and prepared for the Bar, becoming a barrister in 1953. It was quite the feat, especially since their twins, Mark and Carol were also born in that year. She famously sent in her application for the Bar finals while still in the hospital!

Aside from being a barrister, a wife, a mother to twins and a politically active citizen, Margaret Thatcher was also known for cooking.

Even when she was the Prime Minister, she reportedly did not hire a chef and somehow managed to make time to prepare meals for her husband. Sometimes, even her cabinet members got a taste of her culinary efforts.

Political Rise

For Margaret Thatcher, being a homemaker was not unlike housekeeping a country. Understanding *"the problems of running a home"* can bring one closer to *"understanding the problems of running a country."*

She was comfortable in being both a female, a mother and a leader at the same time. She brought in a type of pragmatic, tough, home-style sensibility to the otherwise lofty position of a politician… and the lofty intentions she had for her country.

Her first television interview, for example, had been with her then-six-year-old twins sitting on the arms of her chair.

From the Shadows

Margaret Thatcher's losses in 1950 and 1951 did not deter her from continuing her pursuit of a political career. She tried to become the Conservative candidate for Orpington (also in Kent) in 1954, but was rejected. It wouldn't be until years later that she finally found her place in the sun.

She could have quit after Orpington, but in 1956, she expressed her desire to be a candidate again. Party selection committees had a hard time conceiving of political victory from a young woman with two kids, but in 1958, she applied for the "safe" Conservative seat of Finchley and was selected.

It was not without controversy and the result was met with dissatisfaction from some corners. But by 1959, Mrs. Thatcher, mother of twins, finally made her way into the Commons as MP for Finchley.

In 1960, she became Parliamentary Secretary at the Ministry of Pensions and National Insurance in Harold Macmillan's government.

The Conservatives lost in the government when Harold Wilson become Prime Minister in the mid-1960s. Margaret Thatcher, however, continued to hold prominent roles within her party, using her fine mind and education in posts working on taxes, fuel and power, and transport.

In 1969, she became the Shadow Education Secretary. With Edward Heath's surprising election victory for the Conservatives in 1970, she became the Secretary of State for Education and Science.

She was regarded as a good worker, an effective administrator. But by late-1971, she had acquired the unfortunate title of "Margaret Thatcher Milk Snatcher." It was not an unjust title because while she was in this role, children did lose access to free school milk. For a time, Margaret Thatcher may have even been, in the words of the newspaper *The Sun*, "*The Most Unpopular Woman in Britain.*"

Her rationale for the move was to make a really relatively paltry savings of £9 million in public expenditure, so that she could protect the more educational elements of her budget. Good intentions aside, the unfortunate title still stuck. It was a learning experience for the politician and she was reportedly miserable for a time.

This was likely exacerbated by her relations with the beleaguered Prime Minister Heath, who held the position from 1970 to 1974. They famously did not get along in the best of terms, partly because she reportedly had trouble engaging him with her ideas. It may also be because of the difference in their political views even if they were from the same party.

Edward Heath was himself a barrier-breaker. He was the Oxford-educated, World War II vet and son of a carpenter, who rose to Conservative Party leadership as among the first in modernity not to have come from the upper-classes. His 1970 win in the general elections was a surprise over Labour, but his time at the head of the country's political leadership was marked by a lot of economic difficulties and political challenge from his own party.

He faced strikes from powerful trade unions, rising oil prices (there was conflict in the Middle East at the time) and inflation. He had to make tough choices too, among them a political "U-turn" that deviated from some of his party's beliefs.

Senior Conservatives on the right-wing side, Margaret Thatcher among them, felt he should not have compromised and/or his compromises were not effective.

Margaret Thatcher's steely resolve and refusal to bend (both a strength and weakness) would always be a part of her character. In one of her most memorable speeches, she was quoted as saying, "*You turn if you want to. The lady's not for turning.*"

Heath fell even further from power with the hits taken by the Conservatives in the February and then the October 1974 elections. Someone from the party seemed bound to challenge him, it was just a matter of who would do it and when.

Keith Joseph was one of these men, who shared some of Margaret Thatcher's views and with whom she had a good friendship. In the meantime, Margaret Thatcher received another high-profile post, shadowing the Department of the Environment.

Joseph set up the Centre for Policy Studies ("CPS"), which revolved around free market thinking. He also involved his friend, Margaret Thatcher. Around this time, she seemed to believe that Joseph would be the Conservative party's candidate.

It was an understandable assumption, and one made by many. That was, until a tactless remark by Joseph regarding babies born to adolescent moms from the lower social classes made the rounds and severely impacted his chances.

Elsewhere, Margaret Thatcher was improving her own. In a shadow cabinet reshuffle under the beleaguered Heath, she found another role with which to shine. She gave a stellar performance in speaking for the Opposition during Budget debates.

But mounting a challenge against Heath would still be an uphill climb for her, if not a seemingly impossible feat. He reportedly responded to Thatcher telling him of her intent to challenge him by turning away, shrugging and saying, "*If you must.*"

Margaret Thatcher's rise to the top of party leadership was thereafter aided by a number of factors. Edward duCann, who could have been another (and perhaps more significant) challenger, did not do so. The person who likely would have managed duCann's campaign, Airey Neave, reportedly had issues with Heath and so offered his expertise to Thatcher. He was the kind of savvy, strategic and well-networked political player she needed on her side. At the end of the day, perhaps some of their members just wanted Heath out instead of actually wanting Thatcher in.

The result was the same. Whatever their motivation, the party allowed Thatcher to best Heath and in another round of votes, other runners-up. She became Leader of the Opposition in 1975.

The Leader of Opposition

By 1975, Margaret Thatcher secured the Conservative party leadership. She was the first female opposition leader in the House of Commons, and she would be in this position for four years.

Broadly speaking, the Conservatives in the Opposition and the Labour in Government held different beliefs on the right approach to their country's myriad of economic problems. For the Conservatives, there had to be less government control, less taxation, less spending and trade union reform.

The Labour party had a number of years with which to give their solutions a shot, while the opposing Conservatives fought for their own philosophy.

Margaret Thatcher didn't do too badly going up against the leadership of Harold Wilson and then James Callaghan after him, but she could often come across as shrill in her performances.

Aside from going against opposing views on the other side of the aisle, she also had to deal with difficulties in managing her own party. She built a relatively moderate shadow cabinet, and had even offered a post to Heath (he declined to her relief). She had also engaged some of the men she bested in the leadership race, William Whitelaw and Geoffrey Howe.

Politics was a battle with many fronts. One had to rise above the other stars in one's own party, outperform the opposing one, and all this politicking comes on top of the actual governance of a country still plagued by economic woes.

In the leadership now with like-minded men like Joseph and Howe, Thatcher tried to envision and enact a solution. Of particular concern around this time were the trade unions, which embroiled the country in the so-called "Winter of Discontent" strikes held in 1978 to 1979.

Along the course of her work at this point of her thriving career, Margaret Thatcher's performances had caught the attention of not only Conservatives and the general public, but also that of a powerful foreign eye. *Red Star*, the Soviet Army magazine, referred to her disparagingly as "The Iron Lady" following a defense speech made in 1976.

Now this was a title she actually liked. The image would always trail her from that point onward. It would even be the title of the acclaimed 2011 biopic about her life, which starred (and secured another Academy Award for) Meryl Streep.

But long before she lived a life crafted for the movies, the Margaret Thatcher of the mid-to-late-1970s worked on securing the position that would make her a legend.

Back at the home front... at around the same time that she was crawling up toward her peak in politics, her more than decade-older husband, Denis, was retiring. His business activities had actually been decreasing for years, while her political responsibilities gradually picked up.

He had sold his company and got decent returns for himself as well as a part in the purchasing parent company's board. But by the mid-1970s, work like this was easing up too.

It was perhaps a good thing. As the husband of the leader of the opposition and later the

Prime Minister, Denis Thatcher was expected to be by her side in many occasions. This was especially true when her job took her to foreign shores or required her to entertain.

Perhaps more importantly, she he functioned as an invaluable sounding board and wellspring of wise counsel for her behind closed doors. Publicly however, he was discreet, stalwart in his loyalty, and made a steadfast companion for so powerful and willful a woman.

"The Iron Lady" at Work

In the late-1970s, the public was weary and impatient following "The Winter of Discontent."

The Labour Party was beginning to look impotent against the union problems and amidst other economic challenges. Perhaps the Conservative campaign, the rather clever

"Labour Isn't Working" line, really resonated too, for the nation was going to try a different approach to their years' long problems.

Labour's lackluster performance helped propel the Conservatives back in power by 1979. Party leader, Margaret Thatcher, landed the role (and record first female!) of being Prime Minister.

From her spot at the top, she finally had the muscle to push harder for her right-wing, pro-business, trade union reform beliefs.

And so the years 1979 to 1989 featured a wide-scale shift away from state-control toward a freer business model. Controls in enterprise, pricing, dividends, wages and exchange were either limited or abandoned. The early results of these and their other efforts at economic policy, especially in taming inflation, were mixed.

An oil price hike, which contributed to an international recession, helped matters not at all. But the government under Thatcher stuck by its restrictive monetary policies. They raised income tax too. Unemployment rose – brutally, and urban riots broke out.

The economy at home already would have been a challenge for anyone (just ask Edward Heath), without difficulties mounted both from within and from without.

Thatcher had to face attacks from the Conservative party, sometimes from her own Cabinet. One of her economic strategies was soundly denounced in *The Times* by hundreds of economists.

From abroad, Thatcher's first term was also plagued by Argentina attacking the Falkland Islands. It was a British territory off the coast of Argentina that had been a point of contention between the two countries. The Falklands War, which would begin with

Argentinian invasion in April 1982, turned the Prime Minister toward international affairs when she had previously been very focused on the domestic front.

"The Iron Lady," however, shone as a war leader. She acted quickly and decisively, and supported her military materially and politically. The Falklands War ended with the Argentinian surrender of June the same year it began – bringing victory and prestige for the Prime Minister and Britain. It also likely brought the Conservatives another victory during the elections of 1983... that, along with some measure of economic recovery.

Margaret Thatcher also had to deal with aggression closer to home. In 1984, an assassination attempt by the Irish Republican Army saw a bomb planted at the site of the Conservative Conference, a hotel in Brighton.

"The Iron Lady" showed her mettle with a speech the next day and the conference continued… even when some of those hurt in the blast had been her friends.

Her second term, from 1983 to 1987, also showed her keeping up with the international community's hardest-hitters at such an important time for global change.

She was a staunch ally of United States President Ronald Reagan, with whom she shared conservative and anti-communist beliefs. Together, they showed a strong Western alliance. She held meetings and formed a friendship with the Soviet Leader, Mikhail Gorbachev and hailed him as someone with whom one 'can do business.' She was also in talks with the China's Deng Xiao Ping, making important arrangements regarding the fate of British-administered Hong Kong and establishing the Anglo-Chinese Joint Agreement.

Political Decline

The road there was painful and bumpy, but the economy was recovering and growing. Thatcher's government had withstood a year-long miners' strike. The country looked like a promising investment again.

Furthermore, the Leader of the Opposition, Neil Kinnock, wasn't quite up to par and ultimately proved unconvincing. The Prime Minister had also become a world player, with close connections to the leaders of the United States of America and the Soviet Union.

Thus, the June 1987 election was still a victory for the Conservatives and Margaret Thatcher. She landed her third term in the office of the Prime Minister, but it would be her last.

"No, no, no..."

There were many reasons why Margaret Thatcher's time as Prime Minister and Conservative party leader were coming to a close.

One of them was that she harbored anti-Euro rhetoric that was not aligned with the views of not just many in her party but even within her own team. Her stance was typified by her infamous *"No, no, no"* response before the House of Commons and European Commission Chief Jacques Delors in 1990.

One of the key figures in her downfall is widely regarded to be Geoffrey Howe. It may be recalled from earlier that she and Howe shared some views on the economy and indeed, he was not just a part of her government but a very influential one. He had even been described as a close confidant to "The Iron Lady."

Howe was at different points of Thatcher's leadership, chancellor, foreign secretary, leader of the House and deputy prime minister. He was also co-architect of many of the economic policies that helped put Margaret Thatcher's name in the history books.

Their relationship soured over their divergent views on Britain's participation in a more centralized Europe. One of the techniques Howe reportedly employed to convince the Prime Minister to do what he believed was the right course of action was to threaten her with resignation. He is said to have done this at one time, alongside Chancellor Nigel Lawson.

Ganging up on "The Iron Lady" (even if she sometimes gave way) did not come without a price. Their relationship and trust deteriorated and she shifted Howe's role in what was widely seen as a demotion.

The relationship seemed bound to sour at any rate, with Howe worried about Thatcher's somewhat confrontational attitude on Europe.

Her stance can probably be best encased by her "Bruges Speech" of 1988. She believed in a future with Europe, and her free enterprise slant was congruent with international economic liberty in a competitive market. But she also harbored concerns over how European supranationalism could come at the cost of sovereignty, especially with the seemingly socialist-leaning direction of the European leadership at the time. In her view, they have just *"rolled back the frontiers of the state in Britain,"* as the speech went. Why would they wish to be similarly imposed upon *"at European level, with a new European super-state exercising a new dominance…"*

It was in short, "*no, no, no.*"

Thatcher and Howe had very different opinions. But where she could be abrasive, Howe was generally regarded as mild, quiet and sometimes even bumbling. He was not an electrifying speaker and did not translate well on television. One politico compared confrontation with Howe as "*being savaged by a dead sheep.*"

But this perhaps made the resignation speech he delivered all the more striking and memorable. It was a brutal, incisive piece that is often thought of as the precursor to Thatcher's own resignation shortly afterwards.

He delivered it with calm conviction, but it was blistering in content. It was a savage takedown and perhaps, as *ITV* called it in 2015, "*the speech which ultimately destroyed Margaret Thatcher.*"

Howe lamented her perception of Europe as a "*nightmare*" and how that view could present "*increasingly serious risks for the future of our nation.*" He also compared her to a team leader sabotaging the efforts of her own members – "*…sending your opening batsmen to the crease only for them to find… their bats have been broken before the game by the team captain.*"

Those loyal to Thatcher thought of the speech as treachery, a betrayal. Others found Howe courageous in fighting for what he honestly believed was right, and in being the first to really stand up against "The Iron Lady" when she was wrong.

Reactions to Howe's speech will probably heavily depend on how one thinks of Margaret Thatcher… If she was right she must have been betrayed; if she was not, a man of integrity had finally found the courage to stand up for what he believed in.

Even years later, this is still being debated.

The Community Charge Tax

What is indisputable is that Howe's fiery (though coldly delivered) speech helped set off Thatcher's decline, and she was challenged for the leadership by Michael Heseltine shortly afterwards. Discontent was at any rate brewing even before then, and Thatcher's anti-Euro rhetoric was just one part of the picture.

She seemed out-of-touch and decreasing in relevance. On the international scene, the Soviet Union collapsed and Cold War warriors like her became regarded somewhat as relics. She had been close with United States President Ronald Reagan, but when George Bush came into office after the Gipper, they did not share the same camaraderie and shared differing views on

German reunification and its place in the European power structure.

But perhaps most damaging was that back home, she wasn't very popular either. In the Community Charge or Poll Tax, Margaret Thatcher had perhaps finally championed one radical and bitter policy too many.

Support for her – and the pols in her party - corroded with a proposed, fixed rate local tax. It was profoundly unpopular in the public and divisive in the government.

Prior to the Community Charge Tax was the "Rates." "The Rates" was basically a tax system that allowed the local council to levy charges on the populace depending on house rental value. The purpose of the Rates was to have funding for community services and infrastructure.

The Thatcher-backed new tax system introduced by the Conservatives basically still collected funds for the same community purposes as the Rates, and amounts were still to be determined by local authorities. The major difference, however, was that the tax would be a flat rate charged to each adult (hence the moniker, "Poll Tax"). It spared students and unemployed from the burden, but was profoundly unpopular for several reasons.

First, it was believed that flat fees benefited the rich and burdened the poor. Second, big families in small homes felt they were shouldering disproportionately heavy charges. Third, because there was a lot of discretion on the local council level, it was open to overcharging.

Public discontent reached a fever pitch in London in 1990, when a protest march devolved into a riot that left 45 policemen hurt and 340 people arrested.

The level of dismay inspired by the new tax system not only created chaos in the streets, it also endangered the electoral prospects of the Conservative party, whose members were associated with the negativity. And yet with regards to the controversial tax, Thatcher seemed unbending and insistent.

This was therefore what Margaret Thatcher – not a particularly warm or loved politician to begin with – was looking at in 1990. An unremarkable international position. Unrest in the streets from an unpopular tax. Divisions in a party that may lose its position of power. Dissent in her own ranks.

She suddenly surprisingly made an easy target.

Michael Heseltine challenged her for party leadership in 1990. She bested him, but with an indecisive margin that still required a second round. The writings were on the wall. Support for her was wavering. It was enough for her to recognize it was time to step down.

Margaret Thatcher as Prime Minister had never lost an election… but she was basically unceremoniously dumped by her own Conservative Party.

She would always be sour on the circumstances of her downfall and looked upon it as treachery, just as many of her supporters do. She was said to be even more angered by was its poor timing. Saddam Hussein had invaded Kuwait, U.S. President Bush was involved in the conflict, and he was beginning to engage with her expertise. She therefore felt compelled to exit the political stage at a time when the country was on the brink armed conflict.

She announced her resignation on the 22nd of November, 1990. She basically cited the following reasons for her departure: party unity, as well as better *"prospects of victory in a General Election*" for the Conservatives, if she stepped down.

She was out of Number 10 Downing Street by November 28th.

Love and Marriage in the Spotlight

Politics can be consuming and as seen above, brutal and sometimes unforgiving. Sometimes, the only safe space a pol can ultimately rely upon is home.

But by its own consuming nature, politics can take a heavy toll on a politician's personal life. In 1995, Margaret Thatcher spoke of how such an occupation could be detrimental to family.

Home life for the Thatchers wasn't all smooth sailing, even before she became Prime Minister.

Sometimes in the 1960s, Margaret's husband Denis had a nervous breakdown. It might have been due to overwork at the family business alongside his drinking; these are at least what he himself had speculated in discussing the incident with a biographer, along with the heavy pressure of keeping his mother, sister and aunt financially secure.

It is not known if his wife's absorbing political work had anything to do with it (he never openly blamed her pursuit of her career), but a high stress job that limited her availability could not have helped matters much.

Their daughter Carol, had spoken with an authorized biographer of her father's dislike *"being married to a politician"* for a time. Splitting up may have even been in the cards, though this is unverified. Denis eventually became more and more comfortable with his role though. A refreshing break and retirement may have had a lot to do with it.

He recovered from his breakdown by taking a two-month vacation overseas, and eventually sold his company to lessen the work pressure while he slid more and more into being a rising star's husband.

This temporary setback aside, for the most part Sir Denis Thatcher played his designated role well. He may have even summed it best when he said a prime minister's consort was *always present, never there.*

He had considerable wealth, preoccupations and achievements all on his own. As a matter of fact, early in the morning after his wife won Conservative opposition leadership in 1975, he was at his office, as if it were any other day. He continued to be busy with directorships until he retired.

He also appeared to have the personality of a man who could handle standing beside or even in the shadow of a powerful woman.

Over time, he acquired a firmer understanding of his role and what was expected of him. He was loyal to her and publicly discrete (he declined interviews), while providing her with counsel behind closed doors. In her autobiography, Margaret Thatcher lauded these same traits in her husband, describing him as "*a fund of shrewd advice…sensibly saved… for me rather than the outside world.*"

What he did show the world though, was that he could approach his role as Britain's first male consort to the Prime Minister with humor and charm. He was known for a bawdy joke and quick, irreverent quips. His wife's position, for example, he had once described as "*a temporary job.*"

He suffered the occasional verbal faux pas too, but was generally uncontroversial. And while he eschewed interviews, he was friendly to the press.

He managed what is widely regarded as a difficult position with easy grace, even when he was often lampooned and caricatured in the press. The millionaire oil executive, if he minded, did not seem to be too riled and even had jokes about his own alcohol, cigarette and golf habits.

He occupied himself as a support to his wife, and was by her side in many of her trips abroad, including those to South Africa and the battlefields of the Falklands. He was also quietly involved in plenty of charities. He was granted a baronetcy in 1990 for his contributions.

At the time of Denis Thatcher's death at age 88 in June 2003, Prime Minister Tony Blair referred to him as kind and generous, "*a real gentleman*." Iain Duncan Smith, then leader of the Conservatives, praised him as "*what was best in the wartime generation*."

But greater and sweeter than any praise from illustrious figures is how *his* "Iron Lady" wife thought of him. The former PM once referred to her husband as the "*golden thread*" wound across her life.

He died at a London hospital, with his famous wife and twin children by his side.

"The Iron Lady" as a Mother

Margaret Thatcher as Prime Minister seemed to have the vibe of a stern taskmaster, not only to the men she commanded but the country she led. One can only imagine what she would have been like as a mother.

We can never really know what goes on behind closed doors, but most can't help but wonder - how could she have been like as a mom to twins Carol and Mark?

It may be interesting to note that Margaret Thatcher herself did not have the warmest relationship with her own mother, Beatrice Roberts.

In the 1990s, Margaret Thatcher released a thick memoir and yet barely mentioned Beatrice, especially compared to how she had celebrated her father, Alfred Roberts. It was not Beatrice's only apparent absence in the politician's consciousness, a phenomenon which became a matter of public (sometimes wild) speculation.

In a 1961 interview, Margaret had professed her love for her mother, even though she also said that, "*...after I was 15 we had nothing more to say to each other.*"

This might have been due to Margaret being a younger sister (to Muriel), with the elder having first command of their mother's attention. It may have also been due to fundamental personality differences that let Margaret identify with her father much better.

Nothing much is known about "Beatie" as Beatrice was called. She was born in Grantham in 1888 to parents Daniel Stephenson (a cloakroom attendant) and Phoebe Crust (who worked in a factory). She was brought up in a strict household and was also a regular attendee at Sunday services.

She had some cooking and baking skills. The skills she shared with Margaret; the food she made she shared with the less fortunate. In latter interviews, Margaret Thatcher seemed to be able to say very little about her, other than that she was a generous, practical woman who kept her opinions to herself.

Quite different indeed from Margaret! So how was her relationship with her own children, given her notoriously demanding work, and the vague relationship she had with her own mom?

When Carol and Mark – twins two minutes apart – were born, their mother Margaret was 27 years old and on the brink of breaking into politics.

It was August 1953, and their mom wouldn't become the Conservative representative for Finchley in North London for a few more years. But she was still busy and not unlike other families of the Thatchers' stature, availed of the care of a full-time nanny.

Parents generally do not admit to favorites and Margaret has been described as a loving mother to both her kids, but it was believed by many that Mark was hers. He brought out a light in her eye and a notable note in her voice.

This reportedly did not escape Carol, who has been quoted as saying, *"Mark was certainly the star"* and writing how she harbored feelings of being *"second of the two."*

Carol seemed to harbor complex feelings about her vaunted mother. She studied law, moved countries and became a successful media personality. She is a journalist and broadcaster, and had also featured in the ITV show, *I'm a Celebrity… Get Me Out of Here!*

But she also believed that her achievements wouldn't be enough for anyone to *"ever know me for being anything other than Margaret Thatcher's daughter…"*

She never felt unloved though. One of the more endearing stories about how Margaret Thatcher could be both PM and mom at the same time was when Carol had a relationship with then-MP John Aitken. The couple made plans to go on holiday, but he was suddenly faced with an important political vote that would have jeopardized their travel arrangements. Carol's mom, Opposition leader at the time, shuffled their political business around discretely for her daughter's sake. Unfortunately, nothing flourished of Carol's and Aitken's relationship.

Carol proved dutiful a daughter too. Even if she felt that Mark was the favorite, she was said to be the one who mostly looked after their mother in Margaret Thatcher's final years.

The siblings had a strained relationship that is said to have escalated into a real feud following their mother's passing.

Carol had arranged for an auction of their mother's things, which reportedly infuriated her brother Mark. Some people questioned Carol's motives, believing the sale to be profit-driven and opportunistic, while Mark worried about the preservation of the

Margaret Thatcher legacy. In contrast to Carol, he was said to have hung onto what their mother had left him.

It was not the first time the siblings had differing views on their mother's legacy and how it was to be preserved. Mark was also reportedly in dismay over some parts of Carol's 2008 memoir, *A Swim-on Part in the Goldfish Bowl*, which contained details on their mother's dementia.

Not that Mark was completely saintly himself. He failed accountancy exams. He acquired a reputation as a playboy. He showed some recklessness; he was missing for days in the 1980s along the course of driving a rally in the Sahara. He eventually became a rich businessman, and while he seems to have achieved the feat cleanly, it was tainted by the impression of several observers who attributed it to his use of connections. Most notably in 2004, he became linked to a controversial coup attempt in international affairs.

In her later years, Margaret Thatcher confided in her official biographer, the journalist Charles Moore, about her more private regrets. Mr. Moore has been quoted as saying his subject worried about having *"failed her children"* or having been *"an unsuccessful mother."*

This is probably one of the few ways the otherwise singular Margaret Thatcher is like a lot of other working women (no matter the career), especially mothers. There is a so-called 'double burden' of being expected to do well at work, without a reduction in expectations from the home front.

In Margaret Thatcher's case, she (perhaps just as much or even more than society) had a lot of expectations of herself. According to her daughter Carol, *"she never relaxed,"* doing household chores quickly so that she could turn to the correspondences and speechwriting required of her parliamentary position. Carol called her a *"superwoman before the phrase had been invented."*

Aside from helping to run a country, Margaret Thatcher was also involved in a litany of more homely pursuits. Among them – cooking for her husband and personally wallpapering Carol and Mark's rooms.

But even if she seemed to have given a fair quantity of her time to family, Margaret Thatcher also worried about the *quality* of it. She reportedly worried about her mental engagement with her loved ones. In her later years, she reportedly feared being elsewhere mentally and thinking on other things, even in the presence of family.

The twins Carol and Mark are not close to each other. Blood relations did not automatically mean closeness after all. As

Carol once said, "*You need to have something in common.*"

Whether or not this had anything to do with how they were raised is unknown. As for their relationship with their mother... In Margaret Thatcher's years of decline, the twins were not a frequent presence in her life. Carol had once said something along the lines of it being too much to expect grown-up children "*to boomerang back*" enough to allow an absentee mother to "*make up for lost time.*"

Margaret Thatcher, who could be very pragmatic, probably understood what her life in politics cost her in the end. In a magazine interview in her later years, she was quoted as saying – "*you can't have everything.*"

She described holding the position of Prime Minister of the country as "*the greatest privilege,*" while recognizing the toll on her family. But in the final balance, she still seemed comfortable about her life choices, saying – *"I can't regret."*

Legacy

Margaret Thatcher had paid the price for her political service and inextricably, political ambition. She made her mark and then was forced down, even as she had already made sacrifices in her personal life. But she still had a lot of life to live after being Prime Minister.

Life after 10 Downing Street

Political image recovery came for Margaret Thatcher when the ERM collapsed and her Conservative successor John Major proved competent in economic management of the country. When some of her concerns proved right after all, she regained standing within her own party too.

Internationally, her star shone brightly as well. She became an in-demand (and extremely well-compensated) speaker at home and abroad.

She also worked heavily on humanitarian concerns. She was outspoken about the genocide in the former Yugoslavia. She did fundraising for The Margaret Thatcher Foundation's variety of causes.

In 1992, Margaret Thatcher made her way into the House of Lords as Baroness Thatcher of Kesteven. Somehow she found time to author several books about her life, her work, and her craft.

Just as the title suggests, *The Downing Street Years* (1993) chronicled her time holding the office of the Prime Minister. *The Path to Power* (1995) was an account of her early life. *Statecraft* (2002) was about international affairs.

She was getting on in years by her third tome, however, and suffered several mini-strokes. She had to back away from speaking engagements due to frail health.

She also suffered a number of heartbreaks around the same time. 2003 saw the death of her beloved Denis, her "*golden thread*" with whom she had been married for over fifty years, since 1951. Shortly afterwards also saw the death of her close friend and ally, former U.S. President Ronald Reagan.

2005 at least saw a celebration, for her 80th birthday. A celebration held in her honor was even attended by Tony Blair and Queen Elizabeth II herself.

Her deteriorating health started regularly hitting the news by the 2010s. She missed her 85th birthday celebration, hosted by David Cameron, at Number 10. She missed the 2011 wedding of Prince William, the same year that her office located at the House of Lords was shuttered for good. She retreated from the public eye, and lived quietly in London with a failing memory.

Baroness Margaret Thatcher passed away in April 2013 at the age of 87. Her death by stroke marked the end of years of struggle with illness.

A Mixed Legacy

When she died, she held the record as longest serving Prime Minister of the United Kingdom in the 20th Century… she was also the only female (she wouldn't be followed by another until many years after her death, by Theresa May in 2016).

When she died, she was greatly mourned. Not just a leader, as had been said by then Prime Minister David Cameron – a savior. She stood up stalwartly against communism. Her "Iron Lady" nickname, it must be remembered, had come from Soviet journalists... and she reportedly liked it. In this and in other ways she was a strong leader. She was certainly perceived as such by her own countrymen too.

After all, she also came into position with willpower and a coherent vision, at a time when her country had firmly declined from empire to *"the sick man of Europe."*

There were strikes and protests aplenty – ambulance services, nurses, electricians and so on – that left a lot of public services paralyzed. Schools had to be shuttered. BBC and ITV were taken off the air for a time. Trash was piling in the streets. The Government was contemplating a State of Emergency.

"There's no future in England's dreaming," sang the Sex Pistols at the time – it was not an isolated perspective. *"Britain is a tragedy,"* opined iconic U.S. statesman, Henry

Kissinger. As for the ordinary Briton on the street? Many emigrated away.

Margaret Thatcher came in with big plans and a strong political will, and helped bring about changes, many of them irreversible. A lot of them worked towards improving the lot of many of her countrymen, even if the remedy did sting for a time and there were and continues to be avenues for error and abuse.

Perhaps at times she was too stern in dispelling bitter medicine to the economically ailing country she inherited. Some of her policies have been described as heartless. She may have also been too idealistic about individual morals and the transformative power of a free market in bettering society.

At any rate, her loss was mourned but also brazenly celebrated – even hotly anticipated by some corners. Impromptu street parties, chanting and even sharing of cake broke out in some neighborhoods upon news of her death. Many pubs held happy hours, some even hosting Thatcher-era miners who had participated in their infamously drawn-out strike. There was actually a website put up called *Is Thatcher Dead Yet?*, and someone else had established a social media campaign to bring *Ding Dong! The Witch is Dead* (from *The Wizard of Oz*) back into the music charts.

It is unsurprising that she is both so fervently loved and hated.

Margaret Thatcher's politics could be very severe, and she sometimes had a very stark way of looking at things. The miners' strike, for example, she had actually compared to the Falklands War. *"We had to fight the enemy without…We always have to be aware of the enemy within."* And 'enemies within,' she said at the time, could be harder to fight and be *"more dangerous to liberty."* She was talking about miners from her own country.

She weakened trade unions. She suppressed the miners' strike. Some of her economic policies hurt communities for generations. Her term saw a dramatic spike in unemployment. Her policies tore into the British manufacturing industry, and some of the neighborhoods that depended on it never quire recovered. Heavy deregulation of the financial sector proved a risky enterprise.

Aside from economic hardware, the changes she helped bring about have also been blamed for softer, harder to quantify, cultural effects.

Did she help spur a more individualistic culture of selfish, opportunistic people with no care for anyone other than themselves? One with little society or community? Did she leave behind a country more divided, where some people had to be thrown under the bus for her brand of economic recovery through the free market?

If she did, was it even worth it? Did the irreversible elements of Thatcherism succeed and if it did, does it still work?

Since the end of World War II, three massive economic collapses have occurred, all of them after Thatcherism. Pundits attribute this to a deregulated financial sector with a decimated industrial base. Britain's industrial heartlands never really picked up again, to the continuing detriment of some communities.

Decreased trade union power, which stemmed from anti-union laws and high unemployment, decreased the bargaining power of workers with many in the working class left poor even when businesses did well. By some observers, the country eventually became more unequal, and this is the unfortunate reality lived by many today.

Margaret Thatcher was also on the wrong side of history on a number of international issues. She likened the South Africa apartheid fighters, the Africa National Congress to terrorists and did not support sanctions on the apartheid state. She also received criticism for entertaining alleged Chilean human rights abuser, General Augusto Pinochet, in London.

Margaret Thatcher also fell short of feminist hopes. She was a female, unabashedly womanly and self-aware of her strengths as one. She was female role model, but not a feminist. Her rise was the personal success of an individual who was almost incidentally a woman; it was not a herald of success or a stepping stone for womanhood. Even in an area where she had immediate sphere of influence – her cabinet – she promoted just one female in over a decade. What she did for women was perhaps almost by incident of her existence as an inspiration rather than by her conscious design.

She left behind a complicated legacy. We cannot definitively say how good she was for women entering into politics. Similarly, we do not know exactly if she really saved her country and if her economic and political philosophy is the right one, the right one at the time, or the right one for us now. But that is perhaps the nature of governance. It is dynamic, it can be dirty, and all too often there are no simple answers, no universal solutions, no easy paths. It is not a precise science and yes, mistakes will be made.

When once asked about regrets, Margaret Thatcher had mused on cutting taxes for the rich. *"I thought we would get a giving society, and we haven't."*

She trusted individuals to act upon the same social duties she expected of herself, and they fell short. Her trust in a person's sense of moral responsibility and of individual decisions tempered by a sense of accountability to society and to God, did not adequately consider love of money and wealth, or greed, or accumulation and conspicuous consumption.

If this was her failure, it must also be considered a shortcoming of individuals who could have contributed so much more to the larger society, and did not. It may have been too idealistic to believe in, but it was also a larger human failure that we couldn't live up to that ideal.

Margaret Thatcher has a mixed legacy that in this day and age is still debated. She is not likely to mind it. She was, after all, once quoted as saying:

"If you just set out to be liked, you would be prepared to compromise on anything at any time, and you would achieve nothing."

She was and is not universally liked, a fact which was probably well-known to her when she was alive. But what even her detractors could not doubt, was that she was a woman of steely conviction, commitment and action.

For all of its good and bad, she was indeed a true "Iron Lady."

Printed in Great Britain
by Amazon